{ # Words of Knowledge }

RANDY CLARK

Global Awakening
1451 Clark Street
Mechanicsburg, PA 17055

Third Printing: May 2012

For more information on how to order this book or any of the other materials that Global Awakening offers, please contact:

Global Awakening
1451 Clark Street
Mechanicsburg, PA 17055

1-866-AWAKENING

www.globalawakening.com

Global Awakening
{ Core Message Series }

It is our desire to bring the messages of the Kingdom to the people of God. We have taken what we consider to be core messages from Randy Clark's sermons and schools and printed some of them in booklet form. We hope this teaching increases your understanding of God's purposes for the times we are in and that you find yourself encouraged in your faith. Other core messages are available and they are listed at the end of this booklet.

Table of Contents

{ Words of Knowledge }

INTRODUCTION

In I Corinthians chapter 12, Paul mentions the different gifts of the Spirit, one of which in the NIV is called the "message of knowledge." In many other translations it is called the "word of knowledge." You may ask, "Well, what is a word of knowledge?" That is what I want to clarify for you and expound upon in this booklet. I am going to tell you how you can recognize a word of knowledge in your own life as well as how to give them. I want to add here that these will not be the only ways you can receive words of knowledge. This is just the foundational list that I learned, on ways that a person can receive words of knowledge.

This is not meant to be a definitive study. What I am going to give you is based upon a sociological type study of many people who have moved in this gift. Thousands of people who have received accurate words of knowledge were asked, "How did you have that? How did it happen?" I will be sharing with you the pilgrimage that I have had in regard to the word of knowledge and the fruit of many years of study pertaining to this important gift.

Let's begin out study in I Corinthians 12 beginning in verse 7:

> "Now to each one the manifestation of the Spirit is given for the common good. To one there is given through the Spirit the message (word) of wisdom, to another the message (word) of knowledge by means of the same Spirit, to another faith by the same Spirit, to another gifts of healing by that one Spirit, to another miraculous powers, to another prophesy, to another the ability to distinguish between spirits, to another the ability to speak in different kinds of tongues, and to still another the interpretation of tongues. All these are the work of one and the same Spirit, and He gives them to each man, just as He determines."

What is a word of knowledge? A word of knowledge is a supernatural revelation of information that is given by the Holy Spirit. It is not something that the person who gets the word knows by their own senses, rather, it is supernaturally revealed by the Holy Spirit. I can't say see someone walking down the street with a cast on their leg and say, "The Lord tells me that you have something wrong with your leg." Something like that would be ridiculous! You get receive a word that God wants to heal that person, but not that something is wrong with their leg.

It has to be supernaturally revealed in order to be a gift of the Spirit. Something that is known by natural intuition cannot be revealed by the Spirit. That is because you perceived it from your five senses. It has to be something that you are totally unaware of in order to be a word of knowledge.

Many of the examples that will be used in this booklet in relation to words of knowledge will be in the context of physical healing. The Holy Spirit often gives a revelatory word of knowledge concerning the need of a person (or more than one person) for healing. This is an indication that God wishes to heal the person or those who have the condition revealed in the word of knowledge, and usually that He wishes to heal him or them at the time the word is given. When understood in this way, a word of knowledge builds faith in the person who needs the healing and also in the person who received the word of knowledge. Accordingly, the person who received the word should normally speak it out at the time received or at the next appropriate time. Share the word in order to see if it applies to someone present, and if does offer to pray at once for that person's healing.

As you study words of knowledge, keep in mind that they do not have to be in the context of physical healing. Many times the Holy Spirit will reveal different things about a person to bring healing and deliverance either physically, emotionally or spiritually. Sometimes He will reveal sins in a person's life in order to bring freedom. At other times He will reveal different words in order to bring joy or encouragement to the individual. Make sure you don't limit words of knowledge to just physical healing; rather, be open to whatever the Holy Spirit wants to reveal to you about an individual.

Now let me share with you how I came into an understanding of this gift and how it operates.

MY STORY

In this short chapter I want to begin by sharing with you my story of how the Lord began to reveal to me about the subject of words of knowledge. It didn't come with God speaking from heaven with a mighty voice, but it began with a phone call and a man named Lance Pittluck.

Discovering how to have words of knowledge is actually the most amazing thing that happened for me and my ministry. This simple list literally revolutionized my life as a pastor. In 1984 I was pastoring one of those churches where the deacon, Dave, and his wife seemed to be related to 99% of everyone in the congregation. Almost everyone in the church was related—at least as a third cousin. Most of the people were either guards for the Federal Penitentiary, which is a correctional center in Marion, Illinois, or they had rough jobs as coal miners. I had one or two people who had white-collar jobs, and the rest of them were all coal miners or correctional officers.

I had a woman in our church who, together with her sister, had taken care of the children's ministry for about 35 years. This couple was in their sixties. It was a poorly educated congregation, and I remember this woman was related to almost everyone in the church, but she was dying of cancer. We had been praying and were it seemed that we were not getting anywhere, and she seemed to be going downhill – fast. Because of that, I became very desperate. I knew we had a team that was coming out from the Anaheim Vineyard to my little Baptist church. I'd never heard them speak, but God led me to call them and ask them to come out; however, it was going to be months before they would get there. I said, "I can't wait until they get here for the training on healing." So I decided to call them and said, "Is there anything you can tell me over the phone?" I remember that I got a hold of a guy who is now the senior pastor of the Anaheim Vineyard in California. His name was Lance Pittluck. He had been trained and educated as a Presbyterian and was very intelligent.

Lance was doing an internship at the time when I got in touch with him. Lance asked, "Randy, do you believe in words of knowledge?"
"Yes."
"Do you know what they are?"
"No."
"Do you know how to have them? Do you know how to recognize when you're receiving one?"
"No, but I believe in them, because the Bible talks about them in I Corinthians 12." I believed in the Bible, so that means that I believed in words of knowledge. God had spoken to me concerning the reality of the spiritual gifts although I didn't know how to move in them.

We had just built a new education building in the Baptist church I was pastoring. I was sitting in my office at my new desk thinking about the new facility which I was really pleased with. I leaned back and said, "O God, I thank You that I am not a liberal. I believe that You really did the supernatural things in the scripture. And, God, I thank You that I'm not a cessationist. I believe that You still can do them."

I was waiting for that anointing – for that "Amen, Hallelujah" to come – for some evidence of how pleased God was with me. Instead God spoke to me in a way that I didn't expect. I knew it was the Lord, because it was the opposite of what I was thinking. I felt in my heart that I was being quite the Pharisee.

It shocked me because God responded clear as day in my head and said, "So what!"
"What do you mean, 'So what?'"
Then the Lord spoke to me again and said, "You might as well be a liberal or a cessationist when you say you believe that I, God, can do these things because you do not know how to move in them."

That shook me to my very foundation and so I began a quest. Over the next few weeks I bought over $700 worth of books, which in 1983 was a lot of money for me. I began to read and study everything I could find on the gifts of the Spirit and the baptism of the Spirit. I read everything from the "Faith Camp" to the Catholics, to the Charismatics, and even the Episcopalians. I started reading everything that I could get my hands on. In the course of my pursuit of understanding healing, I was told I ought to get a hold of John Wimber. I had contacted his ministry and arranged for a conference at my church, but I needed help now.

I called out to the Anaheim Vineyard and was talking to Lance when he said, "Well, I'm going to tell you how they come, and you write them down." And so that is exactly what I did. I am going to give you that list of the five ways to receive words of knowledge. On top of the five ways that Lance gave to me, I'm going to share two more ways that I've learned over the years since I've been moving in this gift on a regular basis. Please, do not lose this list of the seven ways of receiving words of knowledge. They are very important. This list can revolutionize your expectation of how God uses "little-ole-mes". God not only chooses "little-ole-mes" for healing, but He will choose "little-ole-mes" to receive words of knowledge as well.

In the next chapter I'll share with you the first way that Lance told me how I can receive a word of knowledge.

FEEL IT

The first way to receive a word of knowledge is by feeling it. It comes as a physical, sympathetic pain that you can literally feel in your body. It is not a pain that you would normally have on your own. God oftentimes chooses this way to reveal to us what He wants to do in people's lives at that very moment.

I had heard this same thing before. But where? Then I remembered the year of 1983 and a woman named Edna Brown. God had used Edna in my life before, so I knew that she was a woman of God that heard from God.

In 1983 my church won the Evangelism award out of the 250 American Baptist churches in Illinois and Missouri. The night after I received the award I went to what was called the "Charismatic fellowship," which was like denominational suicide at the time. I went, and there was an Afro-American woman there who had a doctoral degree from Eden Theological Seminary in St. Louis, Missouri. She was an American Baptist at the time. Her name was Edna Brown.
I knew that she was a charismatic Baptist, so I went up to Edna, and asked, "Edna, do you have words of knowledge?"

"Yeah."

"Tell me, how do they happen?"

"You check your body out before you go to church, and when you get to church, if you feel pain that is not yours—that's a word of knowledge." So when Lance told me they can come through feeling them, it was like reaffirming Edna's testimony to me.

The second time that God used Edna in my life was when I was getting ready to plant a new church in St. Louis. I was in Dallas Texas praying one time. I had already gone to St. Louis several times and was feeling drawn there by God to start a new church. But I said, "God, I'll not get ahead of You." I had just heard Judson Cornwall preach about getting ahead of God, and I recognized my tendency to do that. I said, "God, I won't even go back to St. Louis unless You give me a Macedonian call from somebody in St. Louis that does not know I'm thinking about going to St. Louis. Unless I have a Macedonian call, I'm not going back. I'm not going to get ahead of You."

I called my wife the next day and she said, "Randy, Edna Brown called."

I said, "Well, what did Edna want?" I asked this because it was the only time that Edna had ever called my house.

"Well, Edna said she'd had you on her mind the last couple of weeks, and yesterday morning she flipped the rolodex open to call someone else, and it opened to your name. The Holy Spirit said, 'Call Randy and tell him he is supposed to come to St. Louis and start something here.' " This was the final "fleece" I needed to go to St. Louis to start a new church.

So, the first thing on the list of how to receive words of

knowledge that Lance told me was that "You can feel them." They come as a sympathetic pain. This is the way that I get ninety-five percent of the words that I get. I literally feel them in my body as a physical pain that I normally don't have. There are other people who never feel a word of knowledge like this – they get them in other ways which we will also discuss throughout the rest of this book. As I get older, I have been telling the Lord, "You are going to have to switch over to other methods. As I get older these pains are less dependable." I have learned something interesting though. When I receive the sympathetic pain it usually releases more faith in me. I believe that feeling a word of knowledge releases more faith because you can actually feel them in your body. When I feel a physical pain in my body, I don't think that it is just "me" as we often do when we get a mental picture or impression of a word. My mind may wander and have some different thoughts, but I know that I don't just get pains in my body for a second and then they go away. That is why I believe that they increase faith in the person receiving the word.

However, this is not to be confused with a gift of faith. With a gift of faith, you know without any doubt it is getting ready to happen, and you speak it into existence. I have only had three gifts of faith – two within the past couple of years. Two of the three times I have had a gift of faith it was because the word of knowledge was so precise and the pain so accurate. I could say with certainty where the pain was and how it actually felt. That causes faith to rise in the heart of the person with the condition so that they can receive their healing.

When I was preaching down at Omar Cabrera Jr.'s church, in Rafael, Argentina, this pain hit me so hard it literally doubled me over and dropped me to the floor. I thought I had been struck with food poisoning and felt symptoms of diarrhea coming upon me. I was not sure if it was a word of knowledge because I've never had one so strong before. I got up and gave it; and out of a congregation of 500, forty-six people came who had that colon problem. We prayed and half of them were instantly healed! I have never had a word of knowledge before that was as strong as that one.

There was only one other time that could be compared to that. Some time ago there was a major breakout of the Spirit at the FM 92-radio station at Vero Beach Florida, and it moved over to the Assembly of God church. Fred Grewe and I were going back down there because God had used the radio broadcast we had spoken on, and the Spirit of God had fallen tremendously. People were getting healed, and bodies were lying all over the radio station from being 'slain in the Spirit'. Because of the move of the Spirit, they decided to move everything that was happening over to the church. These guys at the radio station had never prayed for anybody in their lives.

We had just gotten out of a meeting at the Tabernacle in Melbourne, Florida in the afternoon. We happened to turn on the radio and heard what had been happening. We got on the phone and said, "Hey, we're on our way back down." So on the way back down I was in the back seat of the car, Fred was on one side, and Michael Thompson (who took Jamie Buckingham's place as pastor of Melbourne Tabernacle) was driving.

All of a sudden I said, "Ohhhhhhhh!" as I clutched my chest. They turned around and asked, "What's wrong?"
I whispered, "I can't catch my breath. I'm hurting." I was hurting really bad!
"Do you want us to take you to the hospital? Are you having

a heart attack?"

"No, I think it's a word of knowledge."

Then Michael Thompson just said, "O God, send me telegrams." He didn't want to receive words of knowledge by feeling them after he saw what was happening to me in the back seat of his car!

We got back to the radio station and there was an elderly man who had that had pain in his sternum – the same place that I was having my pain. He happened to be accompanied by his doctor while we prayed for him. All the pain he was having in his sternum was taken away, and his doctor even verified it! I don't understand it though, because he didn't live much longer after that. He had another disease that he actually died of, but that particular thing was healed in that moment.

I don't know and I don't claim to understand some things. As I've said before, you have to learn how to say, "I don't know." Always remember 1 Corinthians chapter 13:9: "For we know in part..." There are some things on this side of eternity that we will never fully know or understand. But we have to learn how to say, "I don't know." Remember the healing ministry is a lot like ABC Wide World of Sports, "The thrill of victory, and the agony of defeat!" There are times of great victory as well as times of difficult defeat – or at least what seems like defeat.

RANDY CLARK

READ IT

The second way that Lance told me you can receive words of knowledge is to read them. You literally see the words spelled out – even sometimes you can see them on people. You literally see words just going across in front of your eyes. For some people, it's like big newspaper headline going across in front of them. For other people it's like ticker tape, like on the stock market, just going across – and they can actually read it just like they were reading. I have never received a word of knowledge in this way before. However, I've talked with many people that have had them this way. It also seems that people who receive words in this way are very accurate when they give them. Here is an example to explain what I mean.

A friend of mine, Blaine Cook – who was the man most gifted in the Vineyard in the gift of word of knowledge, excluding Wimber himself – one day began ministering to a person and "saw" their medical chart. He didn't know what some of the stuff was, but he literally saw and read the medical chart. But because he saw it and could read it, he could give with confidence some of the names of certain things that he has never heard of before. Having a word where you read someone's medical chart will encourage faith in the one giving the word as well as the one for whom the word is for. The more accurate the word, the more faith will rise in the hearts of everyone around to receive all that God has for them.

I was very impressed with the accuracy of this type of word. In fact, in my actual experience, I've never seen a person move in words of knowledge more than Blaine Cook. However, I have read of Pentecostal leaders who moved in this gift more than some of the Vineyard leaders that I know of.

A few years ago I came across a series of books by Owen Jorgensen entitled Supernatural: The Life of William Branham. In these books I read about a man that God used in powerful ways because of his great love for the Lord. In my opinion, and much of the Body of Christ's opinion, probably the most gifted person in the Northern Hemisphere who moved in word of knowledge was this man by the name of William Branham. God used him tremendously in the gift of healing – but, most of his healings came about as a result of revelation, or words of knowledge. God would often give him a word of knowledge about a specific condition in the congregation or for a specific person, and then he would speak out what God was doing so that people would receive all that God had for them. Because of the accuracy of the words that Branham gave, faith rose in the hearts of many, and as a result, multitudes were healed. My friend, Rolland Baker, a missionary to Mozambique, told me personally that he believes that Branham was the most gifted and anointed man for healing in the 20th century.

I know it was reported that towards the end of his life he moved into theological error, even claiming to be Elijah. But after seeing such false reports about myself I have become very leery of reports against men and women who move in the power of God. I now understand, having experienced it, how people who are basically skeptical and who have a practically closed worldview distort what you really believe, or at least greatly misunderstand you. I believe William Branham did not have a teaching gift, and should not have focused on teaching in the last part of his life. He was poorly educated, which caused him to make several theological mistakes. But his theological error does not discredit the way that God used him so powerfully in the gifts of the Spirit. We often think that God will not use you if you don't believe correctly – that is not right. God will use you as long as you have a desire to be used by Him. The facts remain: Branham had a tremendous healing ministry, and that healing ministry came about through the word of knowledge that operated in his life.

I remember one time we went to a Presbyterian church in southern Illinois where I was doing a healing meeting one night a week for ten weeks in a row. The first night there, I had a man named John with me who was very gifted in discerning of spirits. Also, as part of the ministry team going with us, we had a very gifted woman who was from an American Baptist church. We were already to the church, but the meeting had not started yet.

John came up to me and said, "Randy, do you see that guy over there?"

"Yeah, I see him."

"He's homosexual."

"Well, how do you know that?"

"I see the word written across his chest. What do I do with that one?"

"I don't know yet, let's just wait."

A few minutes later the woman from the American Baptist church came to me and said, "Randy, do you see that man over there?"

"Yeah"

"He's homosexual" It was the same exact man that my friend John had just pointed out.

"How do you know it?" There was nothing obviously different about this man that would make you think that about him in the natural.

"I saw the word 'gay' written across his back. What do we do?"

"OK, go get John. You and John go to him and with lots of humility say, 'If we miss this we're very sorry, please excuse us. We are just trying to learn; we're new at this stuff. Do you struggle with temptations to homosexuality?' Just ask him that."

So they went quietly and privately and asked the man if he struggled with temptations of homosexuality. He said that he indeed did. So they decided to take him upstairs so they could minister to him in private. When they got him upstairs to minister to him, my friend John began to get several mental pictures that flashed through his mind. I want to pick up this story in the next chapter because it leads us to the third way of receiving words of knowledge: what we call "seeing them" or having mental pictures.

SEE IT

Let's continue the story about the guy with homosexual temptations. What happened next? Now, John wasn't reading the words like he had at first, now he was receiving mental pictures. This leads us to the third way that you can receive a word of knowledge – you see them – you don't read them, but see you see them.

John said to him, "Did this start with your brother?"

The man replied "Yes, it did. It started with sodomy acts with my brother."

"Was this act by your brother instigated by your mother?"

"Yes, it was. She was the one who instigated the incident. It was a very dysfunctional family. How do you know that?"

"Because as I started praying for you, I saw a little boy and his brother, and I saw the mother standing over them."

You can have words of knowledge by seeing them.

I remember when John Wimber first started teaching about this, he was telling of one of the first words of knowledge that he received visually. He was preaching, and it came time for the invitation for people to accept Jesus. Out of nowhere, he received a mental picture of a woman's breast. He thought it was the devil interjecting a thought into his mind to tempt him or distract him from the altar call. He was trying to rebuke the devil when in the mental picture the breast opened up and there was a tumor inside of it. He then realized that it was God giving him a word of knowledge. He decided to speak the word out, and a woman was there who had a tumor in her breast. She came forward to receive prayer and was healed that very night!

So there are times that you can see them in mental pictures. The most spectacular time of seeing a word of knowledge that I know of happened with my friend John. John came up to me one day and asked me to pray for his business to be blessed. I really didn't want to do it because I wasn't into blessing businesses. But he said he wanted his business to grow so he could give a bigger tithe – and that convinced me! But, even then I still didn't want to do it. As I started to pray for him, the unction came – that anointing where I began to say things that I've never even thought of before. I really wasn't expecting anything – I just wanted to pray a little pastoral prayer then go on my way. But, something happened. While I was praying for his business I literally felt an unction come into my spirit. So I started praying, "O God, bless this man so that he'll be able to give into Your Kingdom; and prosper him and let everything he puts his hand to prosper. And Father, if he doesn't tithe on what he makes on his business and his business makes it, bankrupt him in the Name of Jesus Christ."

About the time I said this, a woman in my church was

thrown backwards and landed on the floor. We found out that she was demonized, and we'd never seen anyone who was demonized before. Prior to this point in my life, I wasn't even sure that demonization was real. I had been taught at the Southern Baptist Theological Seminary that people being demonized was actually mythological. I wasn't even sure if I believed in any diabolical influence anymore. Anyhow, it scared us, and we didn't have the slightest clue on what to do. However, my liberal theological training doubts were destroyed when the demon started talking through the woman's voice, and her facial features began to distort while the pupils of her eyes were rotating out of sequence with one looking to the left and up, while the other was looking to the right and down. I will never forget how bizarre it was when her pupils actually rolled out of sequence. We eventually got her free though.

After she was set free, she went to pray for her 39-year-old cousin who had grand mal seizures. Her doctor had told her that brain damage was occurring every time she went into one of those seizures. So the woman, who had just been delivered a week earlier, and her husband called me on the telephone. They had prayed for her cousin, and the cousin went into a grand mal seizure.

When they called me they asked, "Do you think it's a demon?"

"Listen, let's not think there's a demon under every bush. You go back and pray again. If it happens again when you pray, then bring her in. It could have just been a coincidence, let's not make everything demonic."

So, a few days later, they went back to pray for her. As soon as they began to pray, she had a grand mal seizure again.

They told me about it, so I said, "Well, okay, bring her in."

I want you to know I was scared to death because there were already all sorts of false rumors going around the church and the town. It is not the only time I have had false rumors spoken against me; but there were so many false rumors going through that town right then that it was weird. So I was thinking, "This is a set up from the enemy. This woman is going to come in here. We are going to pray for her, and she's going to have a grand mal seizure and have massive brain damage. It's going to be in my church, and my name is going to be on the front pages, and my name is going to be mud." The enemy was really putting doubts and fears into my mind. Lots of fear was coming against me, and I was thinking – I don't want to do this because in our whole lives we have only had the experience of one deliverance and that was just a few days ago.

I went and got Morton Kelsey's book and Father Francis McNutt's book and was reading everything I could find about deliverance. I listened to a tape by John Wimber on deliverance, and was thinking, "O God, O God, O God, I'm scared. I'm nervous, I'm anxious about this." On the day we were supposed to do the deliverance we all met at the Baptist church – herself, her cousin (who had just been delivered herself), her mother, John the engineer, and me. I was extremely nervous as I got out of my car that day. John arrived just after I did. He closed the door on his new car and exclaimed, "Hallelujah! Praise God! Isn't God good?"

I was thinking, "Do you know what we're getting ready to do? How can you be so happy? Why aren't you nervous? I'm about to die!"

We went inside the church. Eventually she came in walking

with a walker – remember she's only 39 years old. She could only take small, shuffling steps because she had arthritis so bad in her bones and joints – which was terribly painful for her. She had very bad eyesight and was losing the eyesight that she did have left. It seemed like it took her forever to make it up the steps to the church and into the church sanctuary.

We went to her and said, "Now listen, before we pray for you, we are going to go pray ourselves, and try to get connected with God first." I was so scared and nervous. "Then when we come back, I just want you to know I am not going to slap you in the head. I'm not going to yell at you. I'm just going to talk to you the way I'm talking now. If we do use any authority, we're not speaking to you. If there is a spirit, we're speaking to the spirit, so don't be offended." So after I tried to explain, we went over to the altar and knelt down. We prayed two words, and she fell down and started screaming. I thought, "Oh, my God!"

Now here is an illustration of words of knowledge that you can see. I don't want to lose the point in the story. So John walked up to her and said, "You tried to kill me last night!"

People had always told me if we got into this charismatic stuff we'd go off the wall and get nutty and weird. Now I thought, "We've done it. We have stepped over the edge. We have gone off the wall. We are off the charts. What's he talking about—she tried to kill him last night?"

He said, "I know who you are. God told me who you are. I know what your name is, too!"

And I'm thinking, "What in the world is he talking about?"

"You spirit of wind (and he came up with some big name that doesn't make sense) and spirit of fire in the Name of Jesus, I command you to come out of her!"

Now maybe I was imagining it, but we had swinging doors and it sounded like they were popping and creaking back and forth. I thought, "This is too weird for me. I am a Baptist pastor, and I haven't been asked to leave yet." I was thinking "I can't believe what he's saying."

Then he says, "And what about Michael?" When he said the word, "Michael" she reared up and started spitting and screaming. It was so horrible! I am not exaggerating at all! I am not trying to embellish the story to make it sound better. It was truly amazing! Then he said, "And what about Benton?" which was the name of a town about 17 miles north of the town that we were in. She did the same thing – spitting and screaming. "And adultery?"

She said, "I did not commit adultery, I didn't commit adultery!"

"Yes you did, God showed me you did!"

"I didn't commit adultery, I didn't commit adultery!"

"Yes, you did. God told me you did." Let me say this here: now we had not been taught how to give words of knowledge yet. We didn't have any information on how to work with the gifts of the Spirit. This was definitely not the best way of doing it. But he didn't know any better.

She said, "No, I didn't. It was my husband. I caught him with a 16-year old girl two weeks ago, and I wanted to kill him. They were in the garage."

"Ohhhhhh, excuse me, that's right. He didn't say it was you. He just said adultery. I'm sorry."

About that time her cousin pulled John over, and said, "Man, I got to talk to you." I walked over and said, "I want to find out what's going on."

She said, "How in the world do you know all that? How can you know that?"

So John told this story: "Last night in my sleep a hand came over my throat and started to choke me. It woke me up, and there was such a fear in the room that I panicked. I could not move a muscle. All I could get out was the word, 'Jesus'. When I said the name 'Jesus,' it left. Then a light came into the room. Instead of fear there was love. Then I entered into a vision, and in the vision I saw this woman (which we've never met before). I saw her in Benton, Illinois. She was sixteen years old and that was 23 years ago. I saw her. I saw the car. I knew the man's name was Mike, and I saw him rape her." John said, "I have all the details. God gave them to me in an open vision. He also told me that her grandfather was a Cherokee shaman. He would take her down to the hills of Tennessee and put her in a cave with snakes in it and say, 'Don't worry, the spirit of wind and fire will protect you.'" God had given him the name of the gods. He saw it all in the form of a mental picture.

It turned out that this girl had told her cousin and she had told her mother twenty-three years earlier. Her mother said, "I don't want to ever hear this mentioned again!"

That sixteen-year-old girl had stuffed it – stuffed all the anger, bitterness and resentment – and was never able to work through the forgiveness, and she was never able to work through the pain. She just stuffed it, and the bitterness had eaten her up inside. The bitterness and the anger were destroying her. She had also been involved in some voodoo practices. When it comes down to it, she was demonized and needed to be set free. But in that word of knowledge God got right to the root of the problem. That is one of the most wonderful things to experience – seeing God through a gift of the Spirit get to the root of an issue that could have taken years of counseling and thousands of dollars to bring the person to the moment of emotional release so that freedom can come into their lives. That woman was delivered and healed from her grand mal seizures, her arthritis, and her deterioration of vision! God healed her completely and totally! It was so amazing!

However, I had some of my own insecurities. I began to see how God was using the lay people in the church that I was pastoring and it was threatening to me. This word that John had received in an open vision blew me away. It was more accurate and spectacular, in my opinion, then anything that I've ever received from the Lord. This was a "little-ole-me" in the congregation and not the pastor. I started asking God to treat me as nice as he does all the "little-ole-mes" in the churches.

I complained to my wife, "Why does He give the lay people better words than I get? They'll quit respecting me as their pastor. They're more anointed than I am. Why is that? I don't like that!"

"Well, if you had everything Randy, you wouldn't need the rest of us, and then you'd get proud."

Not only is a word of knowledge helpful for healing, but it is also helpful for deliverance as well. I have seen our team working with somebody and get stuck at a certain point with them, and we could not get them any farther in the process of freedom. Then we heard about Pablo Bottari, and how he would come up and after asking three questions, he was down to the root issues and bringing lasting freedom to people's lives. God would give him words of knowledge for deliverance.

So the first way of receiving words of knowledge is feeling them, secondly is that you can read them like a headline, and the third way is to see them – possibly in the form of a mental picture. A coal miner –Tommy Simpson, my assistant pastor in the Baptist church – was also used powerfully in the gift of the word of knowledge. Sandy, his wife, was the assistant Sunday school superintendent and was a special education teacher. In our town, a small town of about 14,000 people, there was one building with these huge brass letters on it. One day Tommy had a word; he just saw it. It was in those same brass letters that were on the side of the building. He read them. Anyone can receive words of knowledge, like you've just seen. The only thing is that you must have a desire to be used.

Let me share something with you for a moment that I believe is going to be helpful for you. We have small groups in my church and we believe that it creates a safe atmosphere where people can step out and feel free to make mistakes. You need to be in small groups – that is everyone needs to be in a place where they can practice and learn. Everyone who reads this, whether you are Catholic, Baptist, Presbyterian, Vineyard, etc., needs to be in a small group or a safe environment to learn. For our church, a small group is the best place to learn how to move in the gifts of the Spirit. They are the hothouses where something can grow fast. That's where we can experiment and train. That's where we create an atmosphere where it is safe to try. An atmosphere where we know we are trying to learn how to move in the gift of the word of knowledge. The small group is where we learn from each other as well. When somebody begins to have a word we ask, "How did you receive that word?" And they'll tell you. We encourage each other to step out in the gifts of the Spirit. Even if we miss it, we say, "That's all right, it doesn't make any difference if you miss it. There's just twelve or fifteen of us here. We're just glad you went for it." We encourage each other in our successes and what may seem to be failures. It's a no-fail atmosphere. Begin in the small group before "going for it" in the large Sunday congregational meeting.

We have always had home groups even in our Baptist church. We had a large home in Illinois and had about 50 people there on one night. Sandy, the special education teacher, said, "There is someone here who's got high blood pressure." Now, there was this guy visiting that doesn't usually come. Almost always it seems, visitors are the recipients of words of knowledge because we don't know anything about them. Once you've become familiar with each other, the supernatural dimension of a word of knowledge is lost if you already know it in the natural. So you need to have some visitors coming to the group so that you can step out more with words of knowledge. This is what can make evangelism very easy. Words of knowledge get peoples' attention. Most of the key leaders in my church came to the church when we had words of knowledge for them; they got healed; and then God added them to us. Now they are in our leadership core.

But anyway—Sandy said "high blood pressure." There was a guy there with high blood pressure, so we prayed for him. He got healed and went back to the doctor to prove that he was healed.

That night I asked Sandy, "Sandy, how did you get it?" (Because there are five ways you can get them. I've only shared three of them with you so far.)

"I read it."

"Where, on him?"

"Nope, in the carpet."

"Where?"

"Right over there."

I sat there staring into the carpet looking for that word, but I never did see it.

Another night we were back at the Presbyterian Church which I mentioned earlier. We were just learning how to receive words of knowledge, and my wife received one. She said, "Kidney." A little girl came up, and we prayed for her. She had a kidney disorder. (This set of meetings went on for ten weeks, one night a week. We didn't know that the little girl was healed until a couple of weeks later.)
Knowing that my wife had no idea what a kidney looked like, I ask her on the way home how she got the word about the kidney. She said "I saw it."

"Well, how did you know it was a kidney?"

"I didn't. I saw something but didn't know what it was. I just saw this thing, and I said, 'God, what is that?' And then the impression came: 'kidney'."

The third way of receiving words of knowledge is by seeing

them. Again, this is not the only way of receiving them; it is just one of the ways. Let us go on to discover a few other ways of receiving words of knowledge that Lance shared with me that day when I talked to him over the phone.

THINK IT

One of the few times I have ever had an impression was several years ago when we were starting the church I now pastor. We were just starting to plant this church, so at the time we were meeting in a school because we didn't as yet have a building of our own to meet in. One day while we were worshipping I kept getting the word, "abortion, abortion, abortion, abortion." It just kept coming repeatedly through my head.

I decided to get up say, "I think there is someone here who has had an abortion, and God wants to forgive you." Now there was a woman named K_____ who had just started coming to our church not too long before this incident. I knew her story pretty well. I knew that she had been gang raped by her sister's boyfriends and that also she was a prostitute. I knew that she was also an alcoholic. I also realized that she was so damaged that the first time she came to a small group when somebody reached out to touch her she said, "If you touch me I'll hit you. Don't you dare touch me! I don't want to be touched. I don't like to be touched."

K_____ was an interesting person nevertheless. She was so

hard because of being so abused and used to being put out on the streets. She even tried to go to church at one time in her life. She had two children out of wedlock, and she and her son went to a little church near where we were. She had gone to the bathroom and rounding a corner, she heard two ladies in the church saying, "What's our church coming to that we let that prostitute and her bastard children in here?" It was the last time she went to church for many years. No wonder she was so hard and calloused.

That word of knowledge about abortion was the turning point that eventually led to her conversion. She went out the door kind of abruptly. She came back in madder than a hornet. "Who told you?" she said.

"Told me what? What are you mad about?"

"Who told you? I want to know who told you."

"K_____, what are you talking about?"

"I'm talking about the abortion. Nobody knows about that. How could you know that?"

I said, "Oh, you're the one. I didn't know it was you. K_____, I didn't know it. The Lord did. He loves you. He wants to forgive you." That was the turning point in her life.

K_____ was also blind in one of her eyes from her early childhood. A few weeks later someone was taking her home to the projects because she didn't have a car to drive herself. Brenda, one of the women in our church was taking her home, and on the way home K_____ started screaming. So they pulled the car over. She got out and was kind of beside herself. Brenda said, "K_____, what's wrong?"

"I can see out of my eye, my blind eye, that's been blind since I was a child. I can see."

On the way home, God sovereignly healed her eye without anyone even praying for her. The amazing thing was that she wasn't even saved yet – God didn't seem to mind. He wanted to pour out His love and grace upon her – and that is exactly what He did!

I also remember the day that she came to be baptized. She repented and said, "I've given my life to Jesus. I want to be baptized." I noticed that she really looked kind of round in front; and I was afraid she was pregnant again, but I didn't want to say anything. She'd just gotten saved, and her past was washed away by the blood. She'd been forgiven by the precious blood of Jesus and His wonderful grace. We would love her through it – no matter what she was going through. We were determined to help her with the baby. I baptized her. She came out later, and she was so excited. She said, "Look at this," and pulled her slacks out indicating there was plenty of room in the waistline. "I had to wear these bigger pants. I was supposed to have a hysterectomy tomorrow. I have all types of tumors in me. When you baptized me they went away, and my abdomen is flat." She was instantly healed in the baptismal water! This was two wonderful miracles that God had performed on her!

We see more words of knowledge when we work with the poor than anywhere else. When we go to the poor and the lost taking food, we see more there words of knowledge for some type of healing there. We try to model it for the kids and for years have gone down into the inner city and into the projects to do power evangelism (witnessing by the gifts of the Spirit). People think, "You guys are crazy. It is totally dangerous down there." I say, "But nothing bad has ever happened." We even take our children there with us. They see what it is like to live in those projects and to stand in urine when you're going up the elevator—if they work—which most of them don't. Most of the time you have to walk up the stairs because everything is in such bad shape in the projects. But no one has ever threatened us. We see their dilemma, and then go in and pray for the sick. There in the projects God would give words of knowledge to us and to our children. It radically changed us as well as them. Sometimes, we go and minister to people, but God ministers to us through them. We have children today who have grown up and are on the mission field, and they say, "I want to thank you that you took us to the poor. I want to thank you that you took us to the needy. I want to thank you that we gave food away, and you taught us to knock on the door. You pushed us past our fear. I thank you for that. God put something in my heart that I can't get away from. I am in the ministry; I am a missionary today because I saw that side of the Christian faith."

You can receive words of knowledge by feeling them, seeing them, reading them, or thinking them – or knowing them by impression. The word 'abortion' was an impression that I received. As I said, I seldom get these types of words. The last one I can think of, I had a real sharp pain in my lower back. When I gave the word a woman in our church by the name of Gail Smith came up. Knowing she had responded to that word I was watching her and the Lord said, "degeneration". I don't trust my impressions too much. I normally trust feeling words now, because that is how I get most of them. Plus, they are usually pretty accurate. But as far as my impressions, I don't trust them too much yet.

So I asked, "Gail is your spinal problem due to degeneration of the spine?"

"Yes."

"God is going to heal you!"

I felt like I had a lot of faith for this – that God was going to heal her. As we started to pray she began to shake and to perspire. She fell forward onto the altar literally trembling under the power of God's healing anointing for several minutes. When she went back to the doctor, they confirmed that she was completely healed by God's power!

You can think them or get an impression in your mind or heart. My friend, Blaine Cook, moves in words of knowledge so much more than I do. Ninety per cent of the words he receives are impressions. The two most common ways of receiving a word of knowledge are feeling them, and thinking them. So you can feel them, see them, read them, think them, and what's the fifth? Remember, I'm actually going to give you seven by the time we're done.

RANDY CLARK

SAY IT

The fifth way to receive words of knowledge I used to call automatic speech, but because of the occult connotations with that I realized that is not a good choice of words. So I decided to call it "inspired speech" instead. This was the fifth and final way that Lance gave to me over the phone that day.

This way will usually never come until I'm praying from someone or talking with someone. As I'm praying for them I hear myself say something that I didn't mean to say or even plan to say for that matter. It is like when I speak in tongues, it bypasses the cognitive part of my mind, and it shocks me that I even say it. I'll be praying for somebody and hear myself say, "And I pray that you'll forgive your brother who stole that $40 from you in 1930," or something weird like that. I'll wonder, "Where did that come from?"

Instantly tears will come to their eyes, and you know God has given you a word of knowledge for them. You don't think about saying it, or even plan to say it, it just happened to come out of your mouth. You actually hear it for the first time yourself when you speak it out. Sometimes, you don't even recognize what you say. You just think that you're praying as you always would. But God speaks through you when you don't even know it. It bypasses the cognitive processes of the brain. This way is not as frequent, but almost always it comes when you are praying for someone or talking to someone.

When I do meetings, I'll oftentimes have a time before the actual message where we explain what a word of knowledge is, and then we pray for the sick in a group setting. I do this because someone said to me that if I'll take time to explain what a word of knowledge is, the people will understand more what is going on, and it will increase their faith to receive from the Lord. It is during these times we hear things come out of our mouths as we're sharing about the words of knowledge.

It was during one of these times that as someone was explaining what they are, that in their example, they talked about kidney problems as well as liver problems. They didn't plan to say it as an example, but it just came out. It turns out that there was a man in the second row of the congregation that had kidney failure as well as liver damage. He was in desperate need of a miracle. We found this out later as he shared with us his situation. We prayed for him, but we didn't see any improvement right there. We don't know why, but we were faithful with our part to speak the word out and pray for the sick. That is all that you can do. You can speak the word out and pray for the sick, but it is up to God to heal the person. We must realize that we don't take the credit if they do get healed, but we also don't take the guilt, shame or condemnation if they don't receive their healing. There are a lot of factors why people don't get healed – and it is not always the faith of the person. I recommend that you read chapter 17 of Father Francis MacNutt's book called Healing for a more thorough explanation on why people don't get healed.

As you can see, the person didn't plan to say it. There was little wonder with the person as they did speak it out – in their mind they said "Why did I just say that?" But there was not further thought given to it. But God inspired their speech to say something through them that dealt with a specific situation in the building that no one else knew about. This can happen with the 'little ole-mes.' If we will be open and yielded to God, then He can use us anytime He wants to. Sometimes we don't even recognize that He is using us, even when He is.

Saying the words or inspired speech is the fifth on list that Lance gave to me that day over the phone when I called out to the Anaheim Vineyard. These were the five that he told me to write down and never to forget. But, in the following pages I want to share with you two more ways that I've learned to receive words of knowledge since the time that I've talked to Lance. I've also talked with many other people that have received words the same way – that is dreaming them, and experiencing them.

RANDY CLARK

DREAM IT

In these next two chapters I want to share with you two more ways that I've learned how to receive words of knowledge. The sixth way to receive words of knowledge is to dream them. Let me explain what I mean by giving you some examples.

One of my friends, an American Baptist pastor, receives words of knowledge from God through dreams. He dreamed that he was going down a two-lane highway coming upon a curve. To the left was a gravel area where you could pull off the highway. Although there was no apparent reason to, he felt led to pull off. A few seconds later a car came around the curve passing a truck on my friend's side of the road. Had he not pulled off the road, he would have been killed. Sometime later he is on a two-lane highway and came to the exact spot on the road. Remembering the dream, he pulled the car off the road only seconds before another car came around the curve in his lane as it was passing a truck in a no-passing zone. Because he remembered the dream, he and his family were saved from a head-on crash. First you have the dream, then when you are in the reality you remember the dream, and it gives you faith to act.

My wife is very visionary – having both spiritual dreams and open visions. I am blurring the prophetic and the word of knowledge here, but we are talking about revelatory, seeing gifts at this point. One time a young man in our church had struggled with alcoholism. He was in his late teens and had already been through two treatment centers for alcoholism. He had since been saved and hadn't touched any alcohol in over a year. My wife, DeAnne, dreamed that he was drinking and she told me about it the next morning. I told her we should warn him that he was about to come under a great temptation to relapse into his drinking. The dream happened on a Wednesday night. My wife was afraid to say anything to him, because at this time we had not discovered that God was speaking to my wife through dreams. We did not understand yet so we did not share our warning with the young man. We let two full weeks go by, and by that time I could not keep from talking with him.

On Sunday after church I asked to speak with him, telling him it was important. I actually told him my wife needed to talk to him because she was the one that received the dream. When he inquired about what, I told him my wife's dream. His eyes filled with tears immediately, and he asked me when she had had the dream. I told him two weeks ago Wednesday night. He shared with me that two weeks ago on Thursday he had succumbed to drinking again for the first time in over a year and had gotten drunk. We asked him to forgive us for not warning him about the plan of the enemy for his life. I told him his Heavenly Father loved him so much that he had given us a dream to warn him not to fall into drinking again. This young man had never known his biological father, and knowing this I wanted to emphasize how much his Heavenly Father loved him. He was deeply repentant and thankful for sharing with what the Lord had showed us with him. Even though we had messed up by not telling him, the word still had a profound affect upon him. The next two times DeAnne had dreams about people being tempted to fall into sin we shared them with those people as soon as possible. They admitted they had been very tempted to fall into the sin DeAnne had seen in her dreams.

Let me emphasize at this point again that a lot of my examples for words of knowledge are for healing. Healing is something that I'm passionate about, that is why I use a lot of examples about that. However, words of knowledge don't have to be for just physical healing. We must understand that God view's us as whole people, and He wants to heal every part of us. Whether we need a physical healing, an emotional healing, a deliverance from demonization, or freedom from sin – God is able to speak through words of knowledge about all these issues. God is not just concerned about our bodily ailments, emotional ailments, or spiritual ailments – He's concerned about us as people. Jesus came to set the oppressed free – to free us from sin and all its effects. Don't be discouraged if you don't receive words for physical healing, but be open to receive words about anything that God wants to speak to you about to bring freedom to those around you.

Acts 10:38 says, "how God anointed Jesus of Nazareth with the Holy Spirit and with power, who went about doing good and healing all who were oppressed by the devil, for God was with Him." And because Jesus was anointed with the Holy Spirit and power, you can be also. God is with you just like He was with Jesus to bring freedom to the captives. So understand that God can use the 'little ole-mes' because of what Jesus has done. It is your commission, through the power of the Holy Spirit to bring freedom to the captives. So the sixth way that I've learned to receive words of knowledge is through dreaming them. God speaks to you at night while you're asleep so that you can act while you're awake. We will look at the seventh way to receive words in the next chapter.

EXPERIENCE IT

Other ways to receive words of knowledge are just bizarre things that can happen. I can't really define this way of receiving, because God is bigger than the framework that we often put Him into. So, I'm going to share two stories about this, but I don't want to limit this to the only way that God can do it.

The first story concerns Carol Wimber – who is the late John Wimber's wife. At the Anaheim Vineyard she was literally hearing a telephone ring but there were no telephones near enough that could be heard there in the sanctuary. She felt that God was showing her that there were some people involved in using the phone in some illicit, immoral activity. She gave the word, and there were some people involved in this activity who were set free because of that word.

The second illustration involves my wife. One day DeAnne picked up the phone to call the office and there was somebody on our private line. She could not get them off of the line. She noticed though that this was not a good telephone call. There was a sensuous, immoral thing getting ready to happen. She finally just hung up and gave up trying to call the office. She had totally forgotten about it until a later point. Later she went to church and near the end of worship, God reminded her of it. All she said was, "There is someone here who is using the telephone in a sinful way, and that's all I'm saying," but she knew more than that. A young man came up and admitted that he was on the verge of committing adultery because of a conversation he had had with someone on the phone. A word of knowledge had revealed secret sins in the local church body. It happened in a bizarre manner, but it was a word none the less.

So you can see that this last way of receiving words covers all the other ways that God will give them to a person that I didn't mention in the first six. We have to remember that God is bigger than we are and has many more ways of revealing what He wants, the way that He wants to. Don't limit God to fit in the way that you think that He is going to speak, because just about the time that we think we have Him figured out, He will oftentimes speak to us in another way. God wants us to be in tune with him, and not just in tune with one of the ways that He gives those words.

HOW TO GIVE A WORD OF KNOWLEDGE

In this chapter I want to explain a little bit about how to give words of knowledge. I want to be very practical because I think that we must know in practicality how to give words of knowledge with the greatest effectiveness. Words of knowledge are a gift of the Spirit and are meant to be used for the edification and building up of the whole Body. But, because it is a powerful gift, it can also bring destruction to people's lives if not used it the right way.

Now, how do you give a word of knowledge? In giving words try not to say, "I know you have this, because God told me." Even if you're 100% sure, try never to say that. If you do, you are modeling something that can be dangerous for somebody that is not 100% sure. We must model humility – that is very important. We must remember that we are human and we can and most likely will miss it from time to time. We are not perfect – remember 1 Corinthians 13:9? We know things only in part on this side of eternity.

Listen to me very carefully – You will fail! I don't mean to sound harsh in any way. But the fact is that if we are if bold enough to step out, we will miss it from time to time.

But it is worth taking the risk to give the words to see God bring great freedom to those that are being ministered to. John Wimber said that you spell 'faith' as 'r-i-s-k.' Faith is not necessarily the assurance that someone is going to be healed – though that is part of it. But faith is just the confidence to even step out and give what you feel like the Lord is speaking to you. Faith is simply obedience and the willingness to risk. We must risk our reputation and lives in order to be obedient to the Lord.

Most of the time when we say things in a really strong manner, it makes us feel more secure and sometimes makes it easier to give the words. I have encouraged my people not to say, "thus saith the Lord." I have encouraged them to say very humbly, "You know, I'm not sure this is God, and if it doesn't bear witness with you, let it be like water on a duck's back." If you are seen to be a person of authority and you are wrong, they may go into introspection and be under condemnation for a long time because they think God is showing them something they are not even aware of in their own life. You may put a curse on people through the words that you speak, even though you may not be trying to. This is truer when the information is about personal issues, than when it is about physical healing needs. However, when you are beginning I still recommend the humble model, and unless you become very gifted in the healing anointing I recommend giving the words with the possibility you might be wrong. Give them with humility!

So, as you can see, we must be careful. Words of knowledge are like TNT— or like nitroglycerine. When it is handled properly it is of great value to the church, and when it is mishandled it will blow up in your face and cause you all types of problems and hurt people. And so I say again, always use humility. Even if you know that you are 100%

sure you are right, don't give them proudly or forcefully. Use a spirit of humility and gentleness. We have already seen too much pride in the church, and we don't want to model that anymore. If you do it humbly, what if you miss? You have already said you could miss. It is so easy in that type of an atmosphere to begin to learn. It is easy to learn to discern when it was right or of God, and when it was not right or of yourself. You have to have an atmosphere where it is all right to make a mistake, and you learn by trial and error. You will learn there are certain ways that God speaks to you and you are very accurate, and there are other ways that you have to say it with a whole lot of humility because you realize there is a good chance you could be wrong.

I want to finish up the story that I started at the beginning about the woman who was a children's ministry worker who was dying of cancer. I called Lance and he gave me the five main ways you can receive a word of knowledge. Now let's pick up there.

I wrote down the five ways that you could have a word of knowledge like Lance told me to. That was between Tuesday and Thursday. On that Sunday we were praying for another man in our church. It was one of those times where we were all praying and holding hands at the front of the altar. You know, those times in church when you pray for people who are not present? That is what we were doing. We were praying for a young man, who was not present but who had a back problem. I have to be honest here: I don't have much faith for that kind of prayer. I mean, you have to be really high up there to be successful in that type of prayer. I admit that I'm not at that level yet. I don't have as much confidence for the distance prayer as I do the prayers where the person is present and hands are laid on them. Don't misunderstand me; I believe God can heal from a distance.

But I also know that sometimes the faith of the pray-ers is very important, and I admit that I have less faith for praying at a distance.

We were praying and I, for one brief second, got a sharp pain in my right eye. Now I was in trouble. I had just heard about how to receive words, and now I felt I had received a word of knowledge. I don't usually get pains in my eye. It had taken me seven years to get the respect of this church and I didn't want to lose it by giving a word that wasn't of God; that was just my own thinking. I was thinking, "God, is that You? God, if that was you, do it again." You know what? He wouldn't do it again! Now sometimes, for some people He does do it again; but He wouldn't do it again this time for me. I wondered, "God, was that a word of knowledge?" I mean, I had just learned about this, and I was apprehensive and was so anxious!

I thought, "God, what if I get up there and say it, and nobody has it?" I literally was scared to death. What was I going to do? Now that I knew how to receive these words, I was responsible to put into practice with what I've just learned. What if it was not God? I mean there was a battle going on in my mind. As we were walking up the steps to the pulpit, I was thinking, "I'm not going to do it; yes, I am. If I do it and I'm wrong, I'm going to look stupid. But if I don't do it, somebody may not get a healing." The bottom line is this: is it worth looking stupid if someone may get healed?
Being the man of faith that I am, I said, "I think there may be someone here who might possibly have, something wrong with their right eye."

An older woman in her seventies sitting in the second row on the right stood up and said, "Brother Randy," (in the Baptist church everybody was brother or sister), "that's me."

Now, I didn't know what to do next. We had not yet been through the healing seminar with the young men from the Vineyard to teach us how to pray for the sick. And because of our lack of teaching, we just didn't know what to do. We only could do what we knew how to do. I said, "Well, come on up here." So, we brought Ruth up to the front of the church so that we could pray for her. I got some oil; I put it on her forehead; and I said, "Everybody come up. Everybody can touch Ruth. Just reach in and put your hands on her and let's all pray together. Let's all pray at once. Let's all pray for Ruth." The reason that I called everyone up to the front was because I wasn't going to be the only one that looked stupid when she didn't get healed. I figured that if everyone came up and touched Sister Ruth, then everyone would be responsible if she didn't get healed and not just me. You know the reason why you pray long when you're praying for the sick and you don't want to stop? There comes a critical point when you stop: you have to find out if the prayer worked or not. You are so afraid that it won't work that you begin to pray for missionaries and everything else that you can possibly think of. Jesus didn't do it that way though. You can see throughout the Gospels that Jesus prayed real short prayers for the sick like, "See." "Hear." and "Walk."

We finished praying for her, and she said, "Whew, Brother Randy, I'm so glad you quit praying for me. I was about to fall on the floor." Now we didn't know anything about being slain in the Spirit at that time. I don't think any of us had even seen that before. I didn't know she was about to be slain in the Spirit because she was under the anointing. So in my wisdom, I told her and the whole church not to lock their knees because it cuts off circulation and you can become lightheaded and dizzy. That is what I thought was going on. You have to remember that I'm a Baptist just starting to experience some of these things for the first time in my life! We come to find out that Ruth's problem with her eye was tunnel vision. Out of her right eye she could only see a small little box of area, and everything else was black outside of that box was completely black. Do you know what? God healed her that day while we were praying for her! Isn't that exciting? I was so excited!

I want to be totally honest and tell you something. I could not enjoy the excitement, because I remembered the pressure of giving the word. All week long I said, "God, I'm the only one in this church that knows how this thing works. That means if You are going to give a word of knowledge, no one else even knows they're happening. They wouldn't even know what it is. You are going to have to give it through me. That means I am the only one in this church that is going to sweat bullets. God, I am a chicken. I am not going to do that. God, I don't want to be the only one."

Somebody said, "Randy, you are so noble. You want to give it away. You want to equip the saints." I want you to know the truth – I'm a chicken. I don't want to be the only one in the church that has got that pressure on him to give words from the Lord. I said, "God, I'm going to tell everybody, then you can use them all." I wish I could say I was motivated to fulfill Ephesians 4:11-12, which indicates that the gifts of apostle, prophet, evangelist, pastor, and teacher were given to equip the saints for the work of ministry. It was not noble purposes, it was just this: I do not want to be the only one sweating bullets that made me to begin to teach other about words of knowledge.

The next Sunday night we switched the service around and I taught first, and then we worshipped second. I taught just what I am teaching you now except without the illustrations, because I didn't have any illustrations yet. I just had, "these are the five ways they come." I gave them, and then said, "Now, let's worship." Then we went into worship, and after worship we had a testimony service.

That very Sunday night during the testimony service, a woman on the back seat who was a brand new Christian – not over two months old in the Lord and poorly educated like many in that church – stood up and said, "Brother Randy, I think I got one of them there things you was talkin' about."

I said, "What?"

"You know, one of them there words of knowledge you were talkin' 'bout. My right wrist is killing me, and it doesn't normally bother me."

I was thinking that I didn't know what to do now. I didn't understand how to pastor this thing. It was all new to me. So I said, "Anybody got a problem with their wrist?" Nobody responded, so I didn't know what to do.

She sat down, and said, "Well, maybe I didn't have one of them there things."

So we went through the rest of the testimony service and were getting ready to have the benediction when Barbara, the wife of my best friend who was a deacon in the church, with tears running down her face stood up and said, "You can't dismiss the service, that's me." That word of knowledge that we didn't think was for anyone was for Barbara!

Barbara was in her early 30's and had already had two surgeries on both wrists. She had plastic pieces put in her wrists, and they were beginning to pop out. She had three children, and this was an area of the community where most of the wives didn't work outside the home. Barbara was one who, like most women then, knitted and crocheted, and she said, "I can't even hardly hold anything—do the ironing, or do the laundry. I can hardly do anything. My wrists are excruciatingly painful."

So I said, "Well, okay, let's pray for you."

We came up and prayed for her, and God healed her! I told her, "If that pain starts coming back, you tell it to leave."

Two days later the pain started to come back so she said, "In the Name of Jesus Christ, I refuse to receive this pain in my wrist, leave!" It never tried to come back again after that time.

THE VALUE OF THE WORD OF KNOWLEGDE

I want to spend the time in this chapter talking about the value of ministering in the gift of the word of knowledge. There is a woman in our church – Ruth, the same woman who had tunnel vision – who found out that the arteries to her brain were nearly clogged.

When I heard about Ruth's story, I immediately remembered a United Methodist woman that we prayed for. This woman told me the first week, "I gotta have my arteries reamed out." While I was at home helping my wife put the dishes away, my right artery in my neck started throbbing. You could actually see it throbbing through the skin. I thought to myself, "What could this be? I was only used to getting words at church; the thought never crossed my mind that you could get them anywhere else. Then I found out you can receive words at home before you even get to church! Because of the throbbing in my neck, I immediately began to think of that woman. On the way down to that meeting that next week—there were a lot of people we were training with us—my left artery started doing the same thing.

This is the first gift of faith I had ever received in my life.

When you have a gift of faith, you pray totally differently. You just know it is getting ready to happen no matter what the outward circumstances or conditions are. I told the people, "Hey, you know that woman who's 70 or 80 years old, the Methodist woman that's been here? God's going to heal her. She needs to have her arteries reamed out, and I know she's going to get healed tonight." Now I never give words like that, but this was a gift of faith!

So we got there, and do you know what? She wasn't even there. Man, I felt like I had egg on my face. I felt shamed and disappointed. I was so discouraged that I couldn't even get into worship that night. I thought so much that God was going to heal her that night. I was walking around, "God, why did you do that to me? God, I looked stupid. God, I thought You said You were going to heal her. Why did You do that, she's not even here?" As I was complaining she happened to walk in – about 40 minutes late. When I saw her come in I ran back to her. I caught her at the door and said, "You're getting healed tonight." I have always taught never to say that, unless you really are having a gift of faith. If you ever do say that, and they don't get healed, don't you put it on them. You must admit that you missed God.

I grabbed her and said, "You're getting healed tonight."

I brought her up on the platform and said, "Everybody watch this!"

I really did; I was so excited! I knew that God was going to do it: it was the gift of faith in operation that night. I had never had a word of faith before. I said, "Watch this, watch what God's going to do to her."

Then I prayed "In the Name of Jesus, I command those arteries to be opened."

Her neck started visibly shaking for everyone to see from several feet away. God reamed her arteries out that night. She was completely healed by the power of God!

Now remember when I said that there are some things I don't understand? Let me illustrate this point further. When we were in Hendersonville, TN, we had a woman get healed of Atypical Idiopathic Parkinson's disease. My mother happened to be at that meeting the same night. She was 63 years old then and needed the same surgery to keep her from having a stroke. I prayed for my mother, and she didn't get healed and ended up having the surgery.

Well, anyway, Ruth didn't want to have the surgery on her clogged arteries until after the healing conference that we were going to have. I said, "Ruth, let's agree. If you don't get healed after the healing conference is over, you'll have the surgery." It was going to be three months after I first found out. She agreed to it. She ended up not getting healed. She had to have the surgery. Again, I don't understand.

When I went to see her I found her greatly discouraged and depressed. She was under a lie of the enemy that so many people with illnesses receive. She felt she had failed God by having the surgery, and that He was mad at her. I could not convince her that God was not mad at her for having the surgery, that she had not failed God and that He still loved her not matter what has happened. She couldn't accept all that. It seemed as it was impossible to get through to her.

All of a sudden, I had this idea. My logic didn't and wouldn't work. All the Scriptures that I knew and tried to convince her of didn't work. For some reason or another, she couldn't receive the truth of the word. Ruth was a tough woman though. She was so tough that she didn't even cry at her husband's funeral. "Tiny" was really a big man about 6'6", and she was one of those women who had worked in the correctional institution. She was close to six feet tall and one of those women who was strong-willed and didn't show any emotion.

I don't understand why I did what I did next. I said, "I can't convince you God loves you, so I'm going to ask Him to come and love you in a way you can feel right now. If you feel His love, will you believe He loves you?"

"Yes."

I began to pray and when I finished we waited about a minute, and all of the sudden she began to cry. The presence of the Lord came upon her in that chair. She was a diabetic, and she had several wounds from the surgery that were truly big. She told me one was in her groin, and another in her shoulder. They told her it would be weeks before they would heal.

As I left and was driving home I was thanking God that He touched her and that she didn't feel like He was mad at her anymore. As I was driving down the road, about 200 yards from my house, I suddenly got a sharp pain in my right groin. I knew Ruth had a wound in her groin, but she didn't tell me in which side of the body it was in. This time the pain hit me twice. I was impressed that the pain came twice because when I asked God to bring certain pains back again, to test and see if it was truly God, they usually don't come again. I put the car in reverse, backed down the road, and went right into her house where we had been sitting.

"Ruth, is it your right groin?"

"Yes."

"God is going to heal you." I ended up praying for her again before I left.

I didn't hear anything about her for a while, but the doctors said it would be weeks before she would heal because of her diabetic condition. My friend Tommy called me three days later and asked, "Randy, have you heard from Ruth?"

"No."

"She said that three days after you prayed for her, she was giving herself a sponge bath, and it was totally healed. It was like baby skin!"

Can you see what I'm talking about? There s a great value in ministering in words of knowledge. Just think about it for a moment. This is not something just for me or for those who are pastors and teachers. The lay people of my church receive words of knowledge all the time – a lot of them more than I do. The supernatural dimension of the Gospel makes the Christian life exciting. The most exciting part of this is that words of knowledge don't come just at church. They can come anytime and in any place. They can come at work, the grocery store, or even when you're shopping at the mall.

I want to give you a word of caution about not using this gift when God gives it to you. You have to be careful with words of knowledge. If God gives you words of knowledge and you don't act on them, you can dry up. We can lose what we have if we don't act on what He's given to us. God will literally give them to someone else. Don't let this put fear in you. God is also patient and will continue to give them to you so that you can grow and become bold enough to step out.

When we were first learning about words of knowledge, we ended up going to a conference. Tommy, his wife Sandy, and I were sitting together in Jim Hilton's church, Lake Country Baptist Church, near Dallas, Texas. Sandy leaned over to me and said "I think there's someone here who . . .." and she told me what she felt that the Lord revealed to her.

"Well, give it! Give it!"

"I'm scared." Shortly afterwards someone else stood up and gave the same word, and it was confirmed.

I want to encourage you to ask God for words of knowledge. When He gives them to you to – go for it, face the fear, and share them humbly. Give God the glory if some good comes as a result, and if you miss assume the responsibility rather than put it on someone else.

PASTORAL OVERSIGHT OF WORDS OF KNOWLEDGE

How do you pastor a congregation that begins to become open to the possibility of words of knowledge theologically? How do you pastor the exercising of this gift within the congregational meetings, the cell meetings, and outside of meetings in the secular context? In this chapter let me mention to you a few things on how to pastor and provide oversight for words of knowledge.

Value of Humility

As already mentioned, we must create a value for humility and naturalness in the administration of this gift. Teach the people to avoid hype, unnatural spiritual tones or attitudes, overuse of authority, and/or Christianeeze. Try to use normal language in giving the words. We must learn to become naturally supernatural. We must walk in a supernatural dimension of the power of God, yet not scare people with our weirdness and excess.

If we look at the ministry of Jesus we can see this illustrated. He was not all hyped up and yelling and screaming at the people who needed a miracle. He was just being Himself. He wasn't trying to hype up the crowd and get them to believe in Him, He was rather just being naturally supernatural to bring freedom to people from the effects of evil.

Tools for Evangelism

We need to encourage the people to see this gift as one of God's tools for evangelism when it is coupled with a prophetic word or a gift of healing. Throughout the New Testament, you can see that Jesus and the early church moved in what John Wimber calls 'power evangelism.' Power evangelism is when the supernatural activity (gifts of the Spirit) come to convince the people that God is present, which in turn gives opportunity for the presentation of the Gospel. Through a demonstration of the Spirit's power, people are drawn to faith that otherwise would not be drawn if there was not power (1 Cor. 2:1-5).

Right Timing

There are two points in the service when I encourage my people to gives words of knowledge. The first is at the end of worship when we have a time for prophetic words. In the church that I used to pastor, we made it a practice to give time for prophetic words at the end of worship. We believe that everything needs to be done in an orderly fashion just like Paul mentioned to the Corinthian believers. Because of that, we don't allow people just to get up anytime and give words of knowledge. We don't need to the let the worship or the message be interrupted so that people can give the words just anytime that they want.

The second time that we allow words to be given is after the time for the invitation for salvation when we begin to pray for the sick. Because of our high value for healing, we had a time to minister to the sick every week at our church. If we want to cultivate an atmosphere for miracles, then we must give time for God to move how He wants to in our services.

Small Groups

I encourage people to expect this gift in their small group meetings. Create a safe atmosphere to "go for it" in the small groups. Help them learn what types of ways they receive with accuracy, and what types of ways are less accurate. This is a place where you are free to learn how to move in the gifts of the Spirit. This is the place for experimentation in my church. It is the place where they learn to receive words, give them and pray for the sick before they go for it in the regular service.

International Ministry Trips

People must have opportunity to minister in these gifts. I like to encourage people to go on ministry trips where they will have many more opportunities to pray for the sick and have words of knowledge. We take many ministry trips outside of the United States every year for this purpose. There is a vicious downward spiral if we don't see miracles on a regular basis. We begin to lower our standard of the word of God and as a result, our expectancy decreases. As our expectancy decreases, so does our experience. When our experience decreases, so does our expectancy. As you can see, you just keep going farther and farther down until you don't expect anything or see anything anymore. I encourage you and your people to go on ministry trips where you will see many more miracles than if you didn't get out of the country.

Other books by Randy Clark

Entertaining Angels

There Is More

Power, Holiness and Evangelism

Lighting Fires

God Can Use Little Ole Me

Other Booklets by Randy Clark

Evangelism Unleashed

Healing Ministry and Your Church

Learning to Minister Under the Anointing

Training Manuals Available

Ministry Team Training Manual

Schools of Healing and Impartation Workbooks

Core Message Series

Words of Knowledge

Biblical Basis of Healing

Baptism in the Holy Spirit

Open Heaven

Pressing In

The Thrill of Victory / The Agony of Defeat

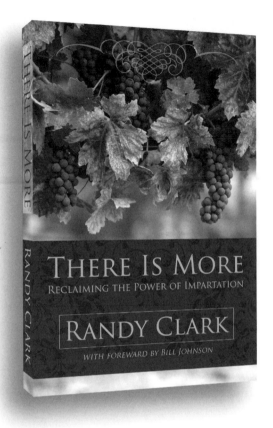

In "There Is More", Randy lays a solid biblical foundation for a theology of impartation as well as taking a historical look at impartation and visitation of the Lord in the Church. This is combined with many personal testimonies of people who have received an impartation throughout the world and what the lasting fruit has been in their lives. You are taken on journey throughout the world to see for yourself the lasting fruit that is taking place in the harvest field - particularly in Mozambique. This release of power is not only about phenomena of the Holy Spirit, it is about its ultimate effect on evangelism and missions. Your heart will be stirred for more as you read this book.

"This is the book that Randy Clark was born to write."

- Bill Johnson

GLOBAL SCHOOL OF SUPERNATURAL MINISTRY

Vision

To release followers of Christ into their specific destiny and calling, in order to live out the Great Commission.

Structure

Global School of Supernatural Ministry is a one or two year ministry school with an emphasis on impartation and equipping students for a life of walking in the supernatural. Classes start each September and end the following May. Courses are offered on-site at the Apostolic Resource Center in Mechanicsburg, PA. Upon completion of each program year a Certificate of Completion is awarded. Students seeking additional educational training may do so while attending GSSM through the Wagner Leadership Institute.

Community

The GSSM student body is diverse in age, culture, ministry experience, and educational accomplishments. From high school graduates to professionals to retirees - the students come together seeking more of God. Supernatural power, passion and honor are key values of GSSM and are reflected in our worship, outreach and personal relationships.

For more information - or to enroll in classes - contact us at
1-866-AWAKENING or apply online at
http://gssm.globalawakening.com

globalawakening

For a schedule of upcoming events and conferences, or to purchase other products from Global Awakening, please visit our website at:

http://www.globalawakening.com